New Baby

PaRragon

Bath • New York • Singapore • Hong Kong • Cologne • Delhi
Melbourne • Amsterdam • Johannesburg • Auckland • Shenzhen

How to Use This Book

 Read the story, all about Alexander and his new baby sister, Ava.

 Look closely at each picture in the story. You may be asked to find or count things in a scene and place a sticker on the page.

 Try each activity as you go along, or read the story first, then go back and do the activities. The answers are at the bottom of each activity page.

 Some pictures will need stickers to finish the scenes or activities. Any leftover stickers can be used to decorate the book or your things.

Mommy and Daddy are home with a brand-new baby sister for Alexander!

Count the animals on the mobile.

Find these things in Ava's nursery.

Her name is Ava. Alexander can't wait to see her. The new baby is very small . . .

Now put Alexander's teddy bear sticker here.

...and very, very...

Find the stickers to finish the picture.

8

Over the next few days, a lot of people come to see Ava.

Can you find these things in the picture?

Sometimes they bring presents for her.
Sometimes they bring presents for Alexander!

Can you find these things in the picture on the opposite page?

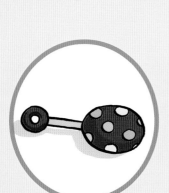

Where is the book sticker? Put it here.

Answer

Mommy always seems to be busy with Ava. "Babies need lots of care," she tells Alexander. "We'll read your book later."

Help Alexander, Mommy, and Ava find their way through the maze to the park.

Answer

In the park, Alexander sees his friend Billy.
"I have a new puppy. He's fun," Billy says.

Find the stickers to finish the picture.

How many dogs can you count?

Can you see these dogs in the picture?

"I have a new baby sister. She's boring,"
says Alexander. "She's too little to play with!"

Can you see Alexander's teddy bear in the picture?

Can you find the puppy sticker?

Find Alexander's cars in the picture.

orange car

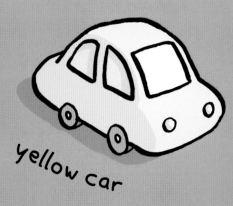

yellow car

blue car

purple car

green car

red car

Back home, Alexander plays with his toy cars.
"Zoom! Vroom!" he shouts.

"Sssh," Mommy says. "Ava is still asleep.
The noise will wake her up."

"What's so good about having a baby sister?"
Alexander wonders. "Ava is no fun at all."

Can you find these things in the picture?

"Being a big brother can be fun," Mommy says. "Would you like to help me give Ava a bath?"

Can you find two ducks in the picture?

Now find the boat sticker.

Answer

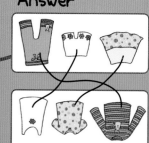

Match the
baby's clothes.

22

Alexander helps Mommy dress his baby sister.
"Thank you for being such a helpful
big brother," Mommy says.

Ava is growing up fast! Now Alexander can help feed her. "Thanks for helping," says Daddy.

Find five differences between these two pictures.

Point to the differences.

Answer

Find the striped elephant sticker.

One day, Ava cries and cries. Mommy rocks her, and Daddy gets her favorite toys. But nothing makes Ava happy.

Find the stickers to finish the picture.

"Look at Teddy dancing, Ava,"
Alexander says.

Ava stops crying, and smiles. "What a good big brother you are!" says Mommy. Alexander smiles too.

Can you find these things in the picture?

"I'm a big brother, and I have big boy toys," says Alexander. "I think Ava should have Teddy."

Put a sticker of Alexander's teddy bear here.

"Ava loves Teddy," Alexander says happily.
"And I love Ava."